A
Woolly Yarn

DEREK THE WEATHERSHEEP

Copyright © 2012 Derek the Weathersheep

All rights reserved.

ISBN-10: 1480229733
ISBN-13: 978-1480229730

All rights reserved, including the right to reproduce this book, or portions thereof, in any form. No part of this text may be reproduced, transmitted, downloaded, decompiled, reverse engineering, or stored in or introduced to any information storage and retrieval system, in any forms or by any means, whether electronic or mechanical without the express written permission of the author. The scanning, uploading, and distribution of this book via the Internet or via any other means without the permission of the publisher is illegal and punishable by law. Please purchase only authorised electronic editions, and do not participate in or encourage electronic piracy of copyrighted materials. The publisher does not have any control and does not assume any responsibility for author or third-party websites or their content.

More from Derek the Weathersheep available, including *Fifteen Grades of Hay* available at www.weathersheep.com

A WOOLLY YARN

DEDICATION

This book is dedicated to me.

DEREK THE WEATHERSHEEP

CONTENTS

1 Birth of a Legend
2 Snatched
3 Dumped
4 A Friendly Face
5 The Dog With No Name
6 The Riggwelter
7 Wisdom from the East
8 The Great Escape
9 A Girl Called Dolly
10 Mrs Honey's Smalls
11 The Spanish Invasion
12 The Jump
13 The Goat Twins
14 Tina and The Bridge
15 A Shot In The Arse
16 Occupy Brecon
17 A Bun In The Oven
18 Onwards and Upwards

ACKNOWLEDGMENTS

There's no-one I'd like to thank apart from myself. I'm the one who has written this book, missing countless episodes of Take Me Out in the process. So I'd like to acknowledge myself.

FOREWORD
by Prof Hans Blipps

I feel a bit of a fraud penning this foreword, especially since TV Weathergirl Ruth Wignall was supposed to be doing it. But I appreciate that she has lots to do with appearing on telly and all that. I also feel humbled to have been asked to write this foreword because I still owe Derek €10. I bet him that England would trounce Wales in this year's Six Nations. Damn that Scott Williams fellow and his chubby little legs.

Derek the Weathersheep first came to my attention back in 2010 when my wife pointed him out to me on Facebook. I thought it was just another one of her Farmville requests, but it soon became apparent that this was a weathersheep of the highest order.

I requested Derek as a friend, as I'm sure you, dear reader, did too. And from that moment onwards, each and every day of my life has been a happier, more pleasant place to live thanks to him. I very much enjoy his witty status updates, but for me, a talent of his that can't be touched by any other sheep is his uncanny knack of forecasting the weather.

Wales is not the easiest place to forecast weather, especially since you've got mountains and things. Throw in the fact that you've also got Port Talbot which creates its own weather system (orange acid rain for instance), and you've got yourself a difficult place to navigate meteorologically. Hats off to anyone who does get it right.

I have been given the opportunity to preview this book, and to my mind, it's the best autobiography about a weathersheep that has ever been put down in words. Nothing comes close.

Derek's tough upbringing has meant that he's kept all four hooves firmly planted in the Welsh soil. I hope he keeps it that way. I don't want to see him in *I'm A Celebrity* this time next year.

Enjoy the book. I'm all paid up now that I've written this. I'm off to buy some new slippers with it.

Prof Hans Blipps
World Weathersheep Foundation
Somewhere in Bavaria
November 2012

1 BIRTH OF A LEGEND (ISH)

I wasn't a pretty lamb.

In fact, most lambs aren't pretty when they're born. They're just a seething mass of blood and fanny batter. Not the sort of thing you'd want to serve up at Sunday lunch time.

But born I was. And with it came the birth of the world's first international celebrity weathersheep.

Of course, Mum and Dad didn't see it that way. In fact, I don't even know who my father was. Rumour had it that God visited Mum in the night and the next morning, she found herself pregnant. As nice a story as it is, I do think it's a load of hairy old bollocks. The more likely version of events is that Mum found herself down the bottom of a field with the girls late one Saturday night, and was taken advantage of by some horny ram. It would explain why Mum was reluctant to feed me after my birth. I don't remember much about my first few hours, but I do recall shivering in a field on my own, and Mum heading back down to the bottom to get a 'bit more of where

1

that came from'. Like us all, she liked a bit of action on a Saturday night after *Casualty* had finished.

Mum wasn't a nasty sheep. Just a bit thick I think. She was just 'one of the girls' – easily led. She'd only 'baa' if the others 'baaad'. She'd only eat grass if the girls were eating grass. She'd never do anything for herself. She only ever did what the mob did. I don't know why she was so lacking in self-confidence. It probably stemmed from her youth. It was something I'd never find out.

So there I was – a tiny newborn, left shivering in the field near a hedge while the cold night drew in around me. Mum was down the bottom with the rest of the mob having a good night out. She had given me only a small amount of her first milk before she had left. Unlike humans, we sheep do not share antibodies with our mothers when we are in the womb. We are basically born without any at all, so it's important that we get some of that first milk to stave off potential infections. I'd only had a few gulps before Mum had put on her lipstick and disappeared. And I was getting very cold.

I do remember looking up at the stars that night. They burned silently and brightly. But all I wanted was the warmth of my mum. I was hoping that one of the other ewes might come over and keep me warm.

No-one came.

I had just dozed off when I heard a snap and crack from the hedge behind me. Like a twig snapping. Then another one. I peered into the darkness but could see nothing. There was definitely something there. But I didn't know what.

What I also didn't know was that my life was about to change within the next half hour.

2 SNATCHED

My head was feeling heavy but I lifted it just enough to see a shadow flitting behind the hedge. There came another crack. I looked out to Mum but she was miles away down at the bottom of the field. Whatever was in that hedge was too close for comfort. I could feel my little heart fluttering with fear. I took in a large noseful of chilly air and tried to stand. Then I heard it.

Whispering.

It sent an icy sliver down my fluffy back.

My head started spinning. Only humans whispered like that. What did they want? Were they coming to take me for their Sunday lunch? Surely I was too young for that?

Again it came. I tried to call out to Mum but my mouth was too dry. My legs were unsteady but I had to get to the safety of the bottom of the field. I didn't look back. Very slowly, and very unbalanced, I began taking my first ever steps. One hoof in front of the other. Then another hoof. Then another. And then another (that's four as I have four hooves).

I was doing it! Once I'd got some momentum going, I was off. I could still hear whispering but it was fading as I moved away from the hedge. Across the field I went. The group of girls were getting closer and closer. I could now hear their chattering.

100 yards to go.

75 yards to go.

50 yards to go.

"Baaaaa!" I called out (that's 'Mum!' in sheep talk).

I had just caught sight of Mum when it came:

A cold hand around my neck.

"Baaaaa!" I called out again. Mum turned to see me but by now, another hand had slid underneath my belly and lifted me clean off the floor.

"Baaaa! Baaaa! Baaaa!" I couldn't get away. Mum just stood there and watched as I was taken back up the field. Why wasn't she doing anything? She simply looked to the other girls for guidance. She seemed to be waiting for one of them to tell her go give chase. But no-one spoke. She looked lost. It was the last thing I ever saw of her as she disappeared into the darkness once again.

***

"Look what I've got!" It was a posh girly voice.

My eyes had been covered so I had no idea where I was, but the slamming of a car door along with the sudden warmth led me to believe that I was inside a car. Oh yes. That's how smart I was. My eyes were uncovered and I came face to face with my captor. A young, pretty girl with two plaits dangling from either side of her head. She took one of them and tickled it my face with it.

"You've actually got one?" came a deeper voice from the front of the car.

"Yes! He's lush!" said the girl, holding me tight on her lap. It was warm in the car. 'Bollocks to Mum' I thought. I'm in a warm car on a pretty girl's lap.

The car moved off, down the dark country lane and on through some villages. I listened to the girl and the man talking.

"The guys back at the house will laugh their heads off!" she said.

"Well they did say to bring one back!" replied the man. I wasn't sure why I'd been taken. In fact, I didn't care. Anything was better than lying shivering in that cold field. At least I was wanted here.

"It's been a great weekend Terry. Thanks for bringing me to Wales."

"That's ok. Never been here before myself. Always thought it was a bit of a shit-hole to be honest, but it was alright wasn't it? They got nice beer and they got nice countryside. Not sure about the funny accents though. I'll be glad to get back to Windsor."

Windsor?

The guy carried on talking in the front of the car.

"I'm knackered. Those last tequilas last night completely wiped me out. I don't even remember getting back to our tent."

Windsor?

What the hell was I doing going to Windsor? In fact, where was it? It sounded mighty posh. 'It doesn't matter.' I kept telling myself. 'I'm warm and having a cwtch.' (Cwtch - it's a Welsh word for cuddle)

I laid my head down and drifted into a deep sleep. I wouldn't be asleep for long.

3 DUMPED

The first thing that hit me when I woke was the smell of shit. At first, I thought I was in Port Talbot.

"The bloody thing stinks! Get it out of here!" The man sounded angry.

"I can't just dump him! I'll take him to a vet when I get home."

"A vet??? Do you know how much a vet costs? We're students! We're not made of money!"

It quickly became clear that they were talking about me. It took me a few seconds to realise that my back-end was cold and getting colder.

"Jesus. What did you have to go and pick that up for?" The man's voice was getting louder and louder. And he was angry with ME.

The scours. I'd heard of the phrase before. I'd heard Mum talking about it to her friend shortly after I was born. Scours is basically having the runs. The squits. The screaming ab-dabs. The shits. I'd obviously 'sharted' all over this poor girl's lap. Wasn't my fault of course. If Mum had given me more of her milk, I'd be less prone to infection. But yes. I'd shat all over the girl. And the back seat of the man's car apparently. The fella wound down his window.

"I can't stand it! IT STINKS!" I could feel the car lurch to the side of the road and come to a sharp stop.

"You've got to get rid of it!" said the man, turning around and leaning over the back of his seat. I could see his face for the first time. A toff lad, with a quiff sat on top of a smooth pebble face. "I'm not going any further until you get it out of my car. There's a field here. You can put it in there."

"I'm not leaving it here."

"Well you can stay here all night then. I'm not going anywhere until you've got rid of it. We're in Brecon. They love sheep here. Some people even marry them." Being called 'it' was really starting to piss me off. Who was this dickhead deciding my fate? It was cold out there. 'Take me to Windsor' I thought. 'It sounds lovely there'.

There was a bit of a stand-off before the girl finally made a move.

She couldn't leave me here! Could she?

Well. Yes she did. The heartless little bitch got out of the car, gently carried me over a gate and into a field. Then she crouched down and placed me on the cold grass.

"Goodbye my little friend." she whispered. She then wrapped me up tight in the yellow towel that she'd brought from the car. There was nothing I could do. Even if I could scramble back into the car, Tarquin or Terry or whatever he was called wouldn't have taken us any further. I had to accept my fate.

The girl kissed her hand and placed it on my

forehead.

"I'm sorry." she said as she stood up. "Good luck." And with that, she tracked back across the field and over the gate. The car pulled away, its engine sound evaporating into the night.

I was left alone. Far away from Mum. Far away from warmth. Far away from anyone.

4 A FRIENDLY FACE

"What the frig is this?" The voice was deep and coarse. A cross between Hugh Griffith and Windsor Davies. I thought I'd woken up in a scene from the movie Grand Slam.

A fat finger prodded my (empty) belly, making me jump.

"Still alive then are we little fella?" I looked up. Beaming down at me was the large face of Farmer Rex Honey. His face was round and creviced and red like he'd been sand-blasted for several hours. But it was a kind face. A big smile smeared across his chops and he patted me on the head.

"Come on lad. Let's take you home."

It was a short journey to Honey Farm and Farmer Honey took me straight into the farmhouse. There, he placed me on the armchair while he farted around in the kitchen. After a few minutes, he scooped me up in his big arms and took me outside where a small washing up bowl was waiting for me. The bowl was steaming hot and full of yellow water. It smelt a bit lemony but still – at least it was warm.

Farmer Honey gave me a good scrub and it was nice to be warm again. I could have spent all day there but after ten minutes or so, I was lifted out and patted down with a warm fluffy towel.

Before long, I'd been cleaned, doped up to the eyeballs with some medicine and plonked into a dog bed in front of the telly in the living room.

"What a lovely-looking slink." said Farmer Honey. He was stood there, arms crossed, looking rather proud of himself. Mrs Honey came up alongside him, also folding her arms and giving me a good, hard look.

"What's he going to eat? He's still a sucker." she asked.

"Dunno. We'll get him on the bottle for now. Then we'll decide what we do with him."

***

I spent the evening in the dog basket in front of the telly. Eastenders was the first TV show we watched. It was the first time I'd ever seen it. Every time Phil Mitchell spoke, it made me want to cough and clear my throat. But I did like him. After that, we watched Emmerdale. Apparently, it used to be called Emmerdale Farm and although there were a few fields in the background of this particular episode, I counted no sheep and no cows. I could see why they dropped the 'Farm' bit from the title.

After that, we watched a film. It was called 'The Neverending Story' although it did finish after just after an hour and a half. 'Clearly a case for Trade Descriptions Act' I thought as I nodded off to sleep.

***

I spent the night where I'd fallen asleep. The embers of the log fire throbbed as the house lay still and every hour, on the hour, the clock in the hall would chime and Farmer Honey would trundle down the stairs and check on me. Each time, he'd check me over, pat me on the head and then climb the stairs back to bed. And every time he did, I'd give a big sigh, snuggle into my dog bed and drift back off to sleep.

'Home at last' I thought. But in the morning, both the dog and Farmer Honey has other ideas.

5 THE DOG WITH NO NAME

"Woof." said the dog (that's 'Who the hell are you and what are you doing in my basket?' in dog talk)

"Leave him alone." shouted Mrs Honey. She was bustling around the house, looking for something. The dog was still stood there looking at me, head dropped to one side.

"Woof." he said again.

'Oh fuck off.' I thought, 'My first chance of a lie-in and you start barking.' I closed my eyes and turned over to get some more sleep but before I knew it, I had a cold wet nose up my arse. What is it with dogs? Why do they always go for the arse?

"Leave him alone!" said Mrs Honey once again. She grabbed the dog by the collar and pulled him away. She dragged him all the way to the door but as soon as she let go of him, like any other stupid dog, he made his way back and sniffed my arse again.

"Get your stupid dog nose out of my arse." I said. He couldn't understand me. I was a sheep and he was a dog.

Farmer Honey came into the room, stopping over my basket. I opened one eye to see his large green wellies.

"Right. Let's get you back to where you belong." he said. With a jolt, he lifted the dog basket, with me still in it, and took me outside to the Land Rover that was idling outside the farmhouse. What was the matter with him? Couldn't he see that I WAS where I belonged? In front of the telly watching Emmerdale?

Mrs Honey came running from the house, tying a scarf up and over her head as she jumped into the car. Farmer Honey locked the house and climbed in to join us. Crunching it into first gear, we rattled our way down the bumpy drive that led to the main road at the bottom.

I was fed up. Why couldn't I stay with them? Here I was on the road AGAIN. God knows where I was going. I doubted it was Windsor. Maybe it was to a lovely place where lots of lambs lived together and had lots of fun and bounced around all day. That'd be nice. Or maybe it wasn't. Maybe it was a vet. Hm. That didn't seem like fun at all. And then it suddenly dawned on me that I might be heading to a slaughterhouse. Oh God! No! Surely to God, no! I'd heard about these places.

I remember lying there, looking out of the car window, taking in what I thought would be my last views of Wales. The beautiful rolling hills, the woolly-backed mountains thick with bracken, and what looked like an old stone house with no roof sat on the side of the hill. And then…..a sign for Pritchard's Farm? But that's where I was born!

The Land Rover pulled up and Farmer Honey headed off to find someone. What was I doing back here? How did Farmer Honey know I'd started my life here?

I didn't want to see Mum. She'd watched as I'd been carried off by that young girl the night before. As far as I was concerned, I had been abandoned. A few minutes later, the car door flung open and a tall, skinny-looking man stood looking at me. His wax jacket hung off his lean frame.

"Yeah. Looks like one of ours." he said before slamming the door shut again.

I looked around the car. Mrs Honey was leaning forward into a mirror, applying her lipstick. She wasn't going let me go with this lanky bastard was she? Mrs Honey snapped her vanity mirror shut and turned to me.

"Right. Let's get you inside."

And with that, the car door opened once again.

6 THE RIGGWELTER

My time back at Pritchard's Farm wasn't a happy one. I never saw Mum again. She had been drafted out with one of the flocks. No-one knows where they went. Most of my time was spent outside in the fields on my own. At night, the rest of the sheep would sit within a pen that was there to protect them from foxes. I preferred to sleep in the field beneath the stars, despite the dangers. They were miserable bunch of sods, always moaning about the weather. But I was beginning to fall in love with the weather. As the spring gradually flowered into a yellow summer, I began taking an interest in all things meteorological. I'd sit there and watch the dark clouds snaking their way up the valley and then watching from underneath a tree as all the other sheep ran for their lives when it started to piss down. All the other lambs were interested in was counting the dags (clumps of dung that clung to the back of a sheep – dangleberries is the human equivalent) on the older sheep.

We had a riggwelter on the farm one day. A

riggwelter is a sheep who's fallen on his or her back and is unable to right itself, usually due to the weight of its fleece. You see the same sort of thing on St Mary Street in Cardiff on a Saturday night. The other sheep thought it'd be funny to leave this sheep there, feet stuck up in the air and to ignore his calls for help.

But I hopped over to see if I could help.

"Baaaaaa!" said the upside-down sheep (that's 'Hiya boy. Do you think you could help me get to my feet here?' in sheep talk)

I explained to him that I was only little and that there wasn't much I could do. There was no way I was going to be able to lift a 20 stone sheep back to his feet. I looked around for inspiration. And it came in the form of the big black cloud that was heading our way.

"Do you mind getting wet?" I asked him. He was a sheep and therefore understood what I was saying.

The upside-down sheep replied that if there was rain on its way, he had no choice but to get wet.

It wasn't long before the wisps of rain that were hanging from the cloud started dragging their feet over the field. As usual, the other lambs were going around, pointing out the dags on the other sheep but as soon as the rain started belting it, they all ran into the safety of the barn.

But for me, the rain was my friend. It started pummelling the belly of this poor sheep. But crucially, it started softening the ground around him. After a few minutes, I started scraping away the ground on one side of him. As the ground started opening up, it was easy for me to get my little hooves right in there and clear more earth. I was motoring. Within twenty minutes, I'd cleared a massive hole right next to the upside-down sheep. All he had to do now was roll himself into the hole and to be upright again. Which is exactly what he did. It took him a few attempts, back and for, back and for, until finally, he rolled right over and into the hole with a plop.

Unfortunately though, he broke all four legs when he fell into the hole. And then the hole quickly filled up with rainwater and he drowned because he couldn't get out. But it was 'the thought that counts' I thought.

***

From my vantage point on the field, summer soon faded into autumn. In that time, I thought about Farmer Honey and Mrs Honey. I thought about that pain-in-the-arse dog and his comfy bed that I'd slept in.

I thought about Emmerdale and I thought about Phil Mitchell. To me that was home. It was where I belonged. From my field, I watched the autumn storms rolling in. More importantly, I started to know when they were coming. A few days before they arrived in fact. Of course, I had no telly in my field, so there was no way I could watch John Kettley and his friends tell me when they were coming. I just knew. I could feel it in my fleece. It was to become an obsession that took me to on to world-wide fame and how me and you came to meet.

But I get ahead of myself. Let me tell you about the curious incident of the llama. He was to change my life.

7 WISDOM FROM THE EAST

I'd never spoken to Dai the Llama before. He'd been hired by Farmer Pritchard to roam the field and protect the sheep. He was a wise old creature but he couldn't defend for toffee. He could spit quite far though but that was no use against a wily old fox. The only thing that he had in his favour was his appearance. He was a gangly, ugly thing. Long neck, sticky out teeth and he smelt of hot arse. No-one went near him. Not even the foxes. And if they dared to, he'd let off this really weird alarm call that would get Mr Pritchard out of bed with a shotgun in a flash. I guess he was quite a lonely creature, just like me. But one cold but sunny day, Dai came wandering over to see what I was up to. He pretended to walk past but I could see his beady little llama eye looking at me.

"Orrite?" I said.

"Orrite?" he replied nonchalantly as he passed by.

"What you up to?" I asked him.

Dai stopped walking for a second. Then he

stopped and looked back at me. Had I said something wrong?

He turned around and walked slowly over to me. For once, he was actually scaring me. He stopped just a few inches from me and lowered his head to mine.

"What did you just say?" he asked. The stench of hot arse filled my nostrils. It wasn't nice. It never is.

"I said 'What are you up to?'"

He quickly raised his head back up. And for a minute he looked to the sky to have a think.

"Sorry. It's just that no-one's ever asked me a question before. I'm not sure how to reply. Give me a minute." he eventually said.

For the following two hours, Dai and I got talking on all sorts of subjects - why we never spoke to the other sheep and why we thought that Mr Pritchard was a knob. Within those two hours, Dai the Llama became my first ever real friend. I told him about my weather predictions and I even told him about the riggwelter. Dai hadn't laughed much but he did chuckle when I told him about that. Dai then told me about how he'd been rescued from another farm in a faraway country. He told me that they sometimes ate llamas where he had come from. But Farmer Pritchard, on holiday, snapped Dai up and shipped him back to Wales. Perhaps Farmer Pritchard wasn't such a knob after all.

Then we got onto my story. I told him about Farmer Honey, Mrs Honey, the pain-in-the-arse dog and his comfy bed that I'd slept in. I told him about Emmerdale and I told him about Phil Mitchell. Dai thought long and hard and then opened his mouth.

"Things turn out best for the people who make the best out of the way things turn out." he said. Or something to that effect. Either way, it seemed like a crock of shit. And long after Dai had trotted off back down the field in the autumn sunset, I started to think about what he'd said. I thought about it long and hard. And I came to the conclusion that I didn't really understand it and was still a crock of shit. I think he was just trying to sound clever.

But it did get me thinking about getting back to Farmer Honey. And it was on the very next day that I came up with my plan to get back home.

8 THE GREAT ESCAPE

It had come to my attention that every Tuesday, an old green cattle lorry would pull up at our farm. It was a battered old thing, like something out of the seventies. And every Tuesday, a large black bull would waddle out of the back and into the field of cows for a few hours. This bull was always smiling when he arrived and as he made his way around the ladies, the driver would slope off behind the barn for a lazy cigarette. He'd always leave the back of the lorry open while he did this.

So when Tuesday came, and while the bull charmed the ladies in the field, and while the driver nicked around the back of the barn for a fag, I took my chance and snuck onto the lorry. I scampered to the back of the truck and hid myself under some tarpaulin. It was a few minutes later that the driver came and shut the back of the lorry up and it all went silent. Except for a few grunts in the nearby cow field.

It was a few hours later when there was a sudden clattering of hooves outside the lorry that I realised

I'd fallen asleep. The back door swung open and the bull thundered into the back. I curled up in a tight ball under the tarpaulin while the back door was locked up and I could hear the bull breathing heavily. Then there was a heavy 'ther-wump'. I dared to poke an eye out to see what had happened. The bull was lying there, knackered but with a large smile on his face. All he needed to complete the picture was one of his driver's cigarettes.

"I love my life." said the bull before promptly falling asleep.

The journey was another bumpy one and I had no idea where we were going. But at least I was getting away from Pritchard's Farm. I was bounced around for about an hour before the truck pulled up and the doors were flung open. I stayed put for a few minutes as the bull was woken up and dragged groggily off and out of sight. When all was silent, I made my dash for it, scarpering off the back of the lorry and into the nearest field where the grass was long and I could easily hide.

To say that I hadn't really thought things through was an understatement. Alright, so I was away from Pritchard's Farm. But now what?

I pushed my way through the long grass until I came to another field which was full of mud. Hm. Normally I'd be relaxing in my grassy field right now. Yet here I was with no idea of where I was. Or worse still. No idea of where I was going.

Scanning the horizon, I looked for some points of reference. I checked the placement of the sun against the mountain range in the distance. Estimating how long I'd been travelling for, and where the sun was in the sky, I calculated that I had absolutely no clue where I was. The only thing that could work for me was the feeling I had in my fleece. I just felt that I had to head due south. It sounded right.

The only problem was that I didn't have a compass. And I didn't know which way was south. I could tell if it was going to rain but Christ knows which way was south.

So I took a chance and followed an old Roman wall for a few miles. If I was wrong, at least I would have some sort of shelter should I need to rest when the weather turned.

Several hours later, I arrived at the top of a hill. I was shattered. My little legs were shaking and I knew that I had to eat. I slumped to the floor and nibbled on some grass, looking down into the valley below me.

Oh my Lord!

I'd hardly swallowed my first clump of greasy grass before I realised that I recognised the small stone building across on a nearby hill. I'd seen it earlier – the one with no roof. I was practically 'home'!

***

"What the frig is this?" The voice was deep and coarse. A cross between Hugh Griffith and Windsor Davies. This time I knew I was home!

I think Farmer Honey was secretly glad to have me back. There were a few little things that gave it away - the cushion placed on the floor in front of the telly. A copy of the *Radio Times* placed in front of it. 'Eastenders' circled in red biro. And a framed picture of Phil Mitchell on the wall near my feeding bowl. He knew. He knew I belonged here.

A WOOLLY YARN

It was as if I'd never been away. And the dog didn't seem to mind either. He found himself a blanket to sleep alongside me on every night. I spent my first winter there. Christmas came and went. The New Year was ushered in with a log fire and a glass of sherry each for Farmer and Mrs Honey, and a small swede for me.

And eventually spring came. And it was that spring, as a young buck, that I first met Dolly.

9 A GIRL CALLED DOLLY

She was pretty but not astoundingly pretty. Not like the ones they show off at the Welsh Show every year. She was alright for 'around the house'.

I still remember the first time I saw her. It was as if the clouds had parted. They weren't clouds of course. They were sheep. They seemed to step aside from the feeding trough to reveal her just for me. I was in awe and had to wipe the dribble off my chin.

I didn't speak to her for a few weeks. I was too shy. But before long, I caught on about her little ways. She'd be up before any of the other sheep. She'd always be first out into the field and always first to the feeding trough. She'd always head up the field at lunchtime for a cheeky dump while the other girls talked about the day's events. I could almost set my watch by her routine. If I had a watch. But sheep don't wear watches.

I knew I had to speak to her. But how?

Fate had a strange way of throwing us two star-crossed lover sheep together. It all happened on a sunny Saturday evening around Easter time.

Farmer and Mrs Honey had been out for the afternoon and so the sheep had free reign of the farm. Whenever the Honeys were out, the sheep would head into the farm house, crack open the biscuit barrel and have a right old' knees up. I'd never attended one of these so-called 'house' parties before. They'd always seemed too wild for me. I guess for the other sheep, they had never really got a chance to see the inside of the house like I had. For them, it must have been a real change of scenery – and even feel a bit illicit dare I say.

One sheep would always stand guard at the end of the field at such parties. Another would stand halfway up the field and another at the back door of the house. This was 'Chain Command'. On first sight of Farmer Honey's Land Rover heading over the hill, the first sheep would say 'Baaaa', which was sheep talk for 'Alright girls, best get your arses out of the house and back out onto the field'. This message was relayed via the two other sheep back to the house in order for the party to stop and for the girls to pile out of the house. Or at least, that's what's supposed to have happened.

On this particular Saturday, the first sheep spotted Farmer Honey's Land Rover in the distance as usually happens. She sounded the alarm to the second sheep stood in the middle of the field. She then called out to the sheep that was supposed to be stood at the back door. But on this occasion, there was no sheep there. The chain had been broken.

I had been watching this from my usual place on the field but it soon became evident that the girls partying had no idea that Farmer Honey and his wife were heading back. And they were making pretty good speed. I quickly realised that I needed to act.

As quick as a flash, I was up on my feet and bounding across the field to the farm house like some kind of sheep-shaped superhero. In the windows, I could see sheep's arses squashed up against the window. The house was packed. With the speed I was carrying, I crashed straight into the back door with a thud. Behind the wheelbarrow that was stood next to the door, I found the missing sheep of Chain Command. She was upside down, off her face on Rich Tea biscuits. Someone had obviously been sneaking them out the back door. I managed to wedge my nose into the door and flung it open.

Inside was a sight I'd never forget.

If you've ever tried to break up a house party in Treorchy, you can probably sympathise with my plight at this point in time. I was faced with scores of girls, most of them up to their eyeballs on chocolate Hob Nobs. There were five biscuit barrels left strewn on the floor, and empty Rich Tea packets all over the place. There was one girl on the floor, passed out. Behind her, there were two girls kissing. And to the left of them, near the telly, was one girl climbing up the back of the settee, trying to reach the Jammy Dodgers on the top shelf of the bookcase behind. It was pure carnage.

I dashed over to the record player and knocked S Club 7 off with an almighty scratch. The room fell silent. A hundred sheep eyes turned to me, most of them blurry or cross-eyed. I took in a big breath, and with all the energy I could muster, I bleated out:

"Baaaaa!" This was the standard alarm call that I'd heard the other sheep using on such an occasion.

One of the girls looked out the window, and seeing Farmer Honey's car heading towards the house in the distance, screamed.

I should have been better prepared for the stampede. I hadn't thought things through again. As it was, there was a sudden rumble of thunder as the sound of sixty or so sheep clattered their way out of the house. Unfortunately, for me, I was still stood by the back door. And I was stood frozen to the spot. I couldn't move. It seemed like a lifetime but in truth, it probably all happened within the space of a few milliseconds. I was knocked off my feet and trampled all over. It felt like a thousand hooves were stamping on me. And no sooner had it had started, the thunder disappeared out and over the field.

There was silence.

Now what usually happens in this situation is that two sheep usually stay behind for a very short while to whip around and clean up before Farmer Honey got back. Biscuit barrels would be replaced and empty biscuit packets thrown away. I opened one eye from where I lay on the floor, half expecting to see the room spick and span, as if nothing had ever happened. Not on this occasion. The house looked as if it had been trashed by a flock of partying sheep.

And it had.

Clunk.

The heavy handle of the back door lifted. I didn't have time to get to my feet before the back door opened wide and Farmer Honey stood there.

"What the frig?....."

His eyes scanned the room, finally falling on me curled up in a ball at his feet. His face went from all smiles to a beef-red huff.

"Oh. You naughty sheep. You are in big, big trouble."

I tried explaining what had happened in the melee that ensued but of course, being a human being, he couldn't understand me. He just smacked me across the arse with a ping pong bat he'd kept above the back door in case of intruders.

***

Later in the day when I was back out in the field, I was sat there feeling sorry for myself. The flock was over the far end of the field, probably unaware of the beating with the ping pong bat that I'd taken on their behalf. I wasn't taking much notice of them. They really didn't seem to care. Except for one pretty woolly head that turned to look at me. It was Dolly.
I could see her as she spoke to the others and a few of them turned to look at me. She said something to them before breaking away from the flock and heading over to me.

'Great.' I thought to myself. 'That's all I need. The girl I fancy coming over to talk to me.'

I quickly closed my eyes and pretended I was asleep.

"Don't pretend you're asleep." I heard her say.

Sigh.

I opened my eyes. Up close, she was even more beautiful than I'd imagined – a long sheep face, with lovely pink ears and the most beautiful pair of yellow eyes I'd ever seen.

"I…we…we wanted to say thank you for what you did back there." she said. I felt shy and only managed to mumble something about how I wasn't a hero, and that it was something that anyone would have done in that situation and that although it'd be nice to appear on the *Daily Mirror*'s 'Pride of Britain' Awards, I never really liked Piers Morgan, and in fact, I thought he was a bit of an arsehole and should never have been given his own chat show after making so many people's lives a misery by hacking phones.

"Piers Morgan left the *Mirror* years ago." said Dolly.

"Yeah. Well. He's still a cock."

"Well I just wanted to say thank you." she replied. And with that, she turned and headed back up the field towards the other girls.

I don't know if you've ever found a sheep's arse attractive. I am sure there are a few humans who appreciate the rump of a nice sheep. But as a sheep myself, naturally, I get very excited by them. As Dolly headed back to the flock, I could have sworn that I'd never seen an arse like it before in my life. Not too skinny, not too wide and with just a little covering of wool. More importantly, it was clean with not one dangling dag swinging between her legs.

There'd be no fly-strikes on this girl.

***

Dolly and I got talking over the next few weeks. She'd come over and sit by me and I'd teach her everything I knew about the weather. I could tell that she was impressed. She'd start coming to me every morning for the daily forecast. At first she'd head back to the flock to tell them what the weather was going to be like that day. But every time she came over, she'd stay a little longer, until eventually, she'd stay with me for most of the day.

It was a different story with Farmer Honey though. He still hadn't forgiven me for trashing his house. I was innocent of course, but he didn't know that. It'd take all my weather-forecasting skills and an extraordinary feat of bravery on a hot summer's day for him to realise what a talent he had on his hands.

10 MRS HONEY'S SMALLS

It had been quite a long, hot summer and it hadn't rained for weeks. Farmer Honey was concerned at the lack of rain because that's what farmers are supposed to do. Something to do with crops and the price of Weetabix or something.

"It's dry as arseholes." said Dolly, chewing on the grass. We often ate out together.

"I know. There's rain on the way though." I said.

"How do you know?"

"I can feel it in my fleece." I said. And I could. I could sense something was going to happen.

Farmer Honey usually checked the grazier's reports for rain. But it hadn't rained for so long that I think he'd given up. He had set about constructing some scaffolding to paint the outside of his house. As anyone who's painted their house will know, rain doesn't help with the drying process. That's because rain is in fact, water.

This one particularly sunny day, Farmer Honey had appeared at his doorway with a pot of paint in one hand and paintbrush in the other. He looked up at the house and started to climb the scaffolding. To the side of the house, Mrs Honey was busy putting out her washing. She was due to attend a Farmers' Wives Gala Ball in the village later in the evening.

But I knew there was rain on the way. I could feel it.

"Stay here." I said to Dolly and trotted across the field.

"What do you want?" asked Farmer Honey from high up on his scaffolding. He'd seen me coming and was now trying to open his tin of paint.

I tried telling him that rain was on its way in from the east but that old sheep/human language barrier was causing trouble again. I had to resort to banging my head on the scaffolding.

"What are you doing you stupid sheep?" I kept banging away, harder and harder until eventually Farmer Honey got so annoyed that he climbed down off the scaffolding.

"Right. What IS your problem?" he asked. I grabbed his sleeve with my teeth and started pulling him to the end of the field. He struggled for a few minutes but eventually gave in. When we got there, he looked out over the hills. There in the distance were some grumbly-looking clouds. And they were heading straight for us.

"Oh my." said Farmer Honey. Within seconds he had scarpered back to his scaffolding to put his painting equipment away.

"Get your washiiiiiiiiing in!" he shouted to Mrs Honey as he headed back. "It's going to piss doooowwwn!"

So Mrs Honey got her smalls in. And Farmer

Honey didn't ruin the paintwork on his house.

Ok. So it wasn't really the extraordinary feat of bravery I was on about in the last chapter. I guess I was just trying to get you to read on. But I did save Farmer Honey's tin of paint and Mrs Honey's smalls. It was then that I realised that I could help the world by letting them know when it was going to rain. I could literally save hundreds of baskets of washing. No longer would people have to put things back on to wash. I'd be saving people money. Saving people electricity. Saving rainforests. Saving the world. I could become the saviour of a nation!

To this day though, I still don't understand why Mrs Honey was so quick to get her washing in. The clothes were wet anyway.

***

I was stood in the middle of the living room floor. Farmer Honey had crouched down so he could speak to me, man to sheep.

"You're a very clever sheep." he said. "In fact, I don't think I have ever come across a sheep with such good meteorological skills as you. I do believe you are even better than that chap on the telly – Derek Brockway. He's always getting things wrong. He's more interested in waving his arms about, speaking Welsh and wearing flashy ties than telling us if it's going to piss down or not. You're my little Derek."

He leant forward and kissed me on the nose.

"Derek the Weathersheep." he said.

11 THE SPANISH INVASION

The coming autumn months gave me a good chance to put my new-found skills to good use. Farmer Honey began relying on me for weather reports. He'd base his weekly schedule around my forecasts. I felt that I'd become a very important member of the farm and before long, farmers from across the region were telephoning Farmer Honey to get the latest news on what the weather was going to do.

It was during the autumn months that we had a new addition to the flock. He'd come from Spain, one of Farmer Honey's attempts to bring a bit of glamour to the farm. He was admittedly a good-looking ram, had a great body and a large and sturdy set of bollocks. The girls didn't know what to do with themselves and for once, I felt that my place within the farm had been threatened. He couldn't forecast the weather but he knew how to get two legs over. Over and over again. After a week, he'd been round most of the girls on the farm.

"Do you fancy him?" I asked Dolly one day.

"I don't fancy him. I think he's good-looking but I don't fancy him." she replied. We'd had a nice day sitting in the field and evening was closing in around us.

"Shall we head to the barn?" I asked.

"Aye. Ok." said Dolly.

The barn was lovely and warm and the girls were settling down in front of the telly that Farmer Honey had installed a few weeks earlier. Dolly and I plonked ourselves down in our usual spot, where our friend Brenda was chillaxing.

"Orri' love?" said Brenda. She was a Cardiff girl.

"Hi Brenda. What you been up to?"

"A bi' of this and bi' of tha' like innit?" she said. "Had Cassanova in yer earlier, trying his luck. I told him – 'You ain't sticking that lipstick anywhere near me sunshine, you knows what I mean?"

Juan the Lovesheep, as the girls were starting to call him, was beginning to get a reputation for himself. Every morning, there'd be some girl complaining that he'd tried to mount her in the night. Some mornings, there'd be complaints from girls who had woken up with his large testicles in their faces.

"Birrova ladies man that one, Billy Big Bollocks." said Brenda." I wouldn't go there though."

Dolly and Brenda had a pretty good friendship and they joked and laughed about Juan before settling down for the evening.

But the next day, I woke up to find that Dolly was not cwtched up next to me as she normally would be. She always used to get up early, but it was still pretty dark.

Brenda was lying next to me. I prodded her with my hoof.

"You awake?"

"No."

"Where's Dolly?"

"Dunno."

I got to my feet and looked around. Plenty of woolly backs lying around but Dolly was nowhere to be seen.

The old wooden door creaked on its hinges as I pushed it open. Far away, over the hills, the sun was just beginning to stretch and yawn. But Dolly was nowhere to be seen.

Just then I heard a muffled sound coming from around the side of the barn. I quickly trotted around and there, to my horror, I found Juan the Lovesheep sat right on Dolly's face. I didn't know whether to shout, laugh or cry.

I stood there for a few seconds in complete shock before Juan noticed I was standing nearby and he jumped back. Dolly coughed and spluttered, and made a few groggy moaning sounds.

"It's not what it seems." said Juan in his clipped Spanish tones.

"Yeah? Well go ahead. Explain away!"

"Well…" stuttered Juan, "It's like this…erm…I've got a bolus up my arse and I was asking Dolly to take it out for me."

"A bolus? What the hell is a bolus?"

"Medicine. It's up my arse."

"Is it supposed to be up there?"

"Yes. But I don't want it up there. It affects my confidence as a man."

I had to stop for a minute to comprehend what was going on. I was arguing with a Spanish sheep about his arse medicine. Meanwhile, Dolly was slowly getting to her feet.

"What's going on?" she asked.

It was clear that Dolly had no idea where she was or what was going on.

"Get over here behind me Dolly." I said. I was quite vexed now. He'd really gotten my dander up. Dolly made her way over to me and then passed on back into the barn. I stepped right up to Juan, nose-to-nose.

"If I ever find you tea-bagging my girl again, I'm going to rip those bollocks clean off you and send them first class to that Chinese place in the village." I stood back, looking him up and down. "Sheep like you make me sick." I said before doofing up some mud with my hoof and trotting off.

To this day, Dolly always maintains that she can't remember anything about the situation and to this day, Juan the Lovesheep has always kept his distance from me.

A few weeks later, I was stood on the outcrop that I enjoyed standing on to watch the weather rolling in when I suddenly heard a voice behind me. It made me jump.

"Long time no see." said the voice.

12 THE JUMP

It was good to see Dai the Llama again. If anything, he could keep an eye on that Spanish lad with the massive bollocks.

Dai was to spend the next year with us as a kind of

watch-llama. It's a bit like a watchdog (not the one with Anne Robinson) but with a llama instead of a dog. He was just like one of us, but with a long neck, sticky out teeth and that whiff of hot arse about him.

He was nice enough though. He was very much into his gadgets. He often wore a pair of night vision goggles when he was out on patrol at night. He also carried with him a cattle prod in case of a stampede. I'm not sure where he got them from but he always had something to impress me with. He was the first animal on the farm to have a laptop computer.

"I can get you one of these if you want." he told me one day.

I took him up on his offer and before long I was able to get in touch with other weather-forecasting sheep across the world. And it was on Friday 17th June 2011, that I joined something called Facebook.

I still remember the first person I asked to be my Facebook friend. It was a guy down in Cardiff. Within seconds of me sending a friend request, he sent me a message:

"Who the fuck are you and why do you want to be my friend?"

Charming.

Eventually though, I gathered a few friends, none of whom I'd ever met but who all appreciated the daily weather forecasts I was putting out each morning.

Friends started telling their friends and their friends starting telling their friends and before long, I wasn't asking anyone to be my friend – people were asking me to be their friend! It wasn't long before I had 100 friends. I felt very popular. But it didn't stop there. Day after day after day, I was getting more and more friend requests.

Then came the odd requests. I remember one chap asking if he could come round 'for a bum'. I laughed it off but then had another one asking when I was free. I checked out his profile. I was rather disturbed to find pictures of him with other sheep. And there were a few of them that looked slightly disturbing. He was quickly blocked.

Then I had a message from a lady who worked in Nantgarw. It's probably best that I don't disclose her name here, but let's call her Mandy Jenkins for argument's sake. I had a few messages from her, asking if I wanted to join her and some of her chums in a dogging session at the top of Caerphilly Mountain. Strangely enough, she looked like she was a Crufts winner.

Blocked.

By far, the strangest message I had in those first few weeks was from a man called Paul. Paul lived somewhere in England, Brighton I think it was, but travelled to Wales regularly on business. I think he was some kind of sales manager and at first, he was very pleasant, complimenting me on my weather forecasting skills and my daily updates. But one day, I had a message from him asking me if I was 'open-minded'. I'd like to say that I was a pretty open-minded person so I replied to him with a 'yes'. A few hours later, I opened my Facebook inbox to find three pictures of him in stockings and a Paul Daniels mask on.

Blocked.

But I was also making lots of lovely friends on Facebook, most of them normal(ish) and with hearts of gold. There were the usual avalanche of Farmville requests coming through (don't you realise that I live on a REAL farm with REAL talking animals? Why would I have time for make-believe stuff like that?) but on the whole I was enjoying finding my way around Facebook.

Dai mentioned to me that I might want to set up a Twitter account. I did try it but to be honest, I had got no idea what was going on. As for Google +…well, I logged on there if I fancied a break from social media.

The problem was, that Facebook was beginning to take up a lot of my time. A few months prior, I had spoken to Dolly about the prospect of arranging a sky dive for myself and the girls at the Royal Welsh Show.

"Will you get off that bloody computer?" barked Dolly coming into the barn one night.

"I'm just telling my Facebook friends about my sky dive." I replied.

"You won't be doing no sky dive if you don't start arranging things."

She was right. With only a few weeks left before the Royal Welsh Show, I really needed to get things planned.

The first thing I needed to do was arrange supplies of parachutes and to hire a plane. Dai was the one to sort this out. I sent him on his way, while I called a meeting in the barn.

There was a lot of murmuring among the girls as I made my way to the bale of hay that I'd put in the middle of the barn.

"Girls…..girls….GIRLS!"

The murmuring soon dropped to a hush and I was able to speak.

"I'd first like to thank you for coming along today.

Now…as you all know, it's the Royal Welsh Show coming up in a few weeks' time. And as we all know, they do the same thing year in year out. A few cows walk around a ring and a few dogs chase sheep. I thought it was time for change. Real change. Time for us sheep to really show what we are made of. What I propose is that we put on a sky dive."

There was a bit of a commotion among the girls.

"A sky dive?" someone called out. "How the hell are we going to do that? We've got no parachutes and no aeroplane."

"Ah. But that's where you're wrong," I said. "We have parachutes AND we have an aeroplane."

There was another commotion among the small crowd stood in front of me. And to be quite frank, I was in fact, talking a load of bollocks. I had no parachutes and no aeroplane.

"But what's the point?" someone called out.

"Because we can." I said.

There was a collective groan and the girls all trouped out of the barn. There were a few mumbles of 'dickhead' and 'arsehole' as they piled out. The only one that was left was Dolly. She stood there looking up at me on my bale of hay.

"I believe in you Derek the Weathersheep." she said.

***

A few days later, Dai had managed to get hold of a parachute for me.

"Now what you need to remember is that if the parachute fails for any reason, you're going to need to curl up in a ball and hope that you land directly on a soft cushion of some sort." he said as he buckled me in. "There. All strapped in. Now go over to that bale of hay there and we'll start practising the jump."

The parachute was heavy on my back and I struggled to climb on to the bale.

"Right. I've seen them do this in *Saving Private Ryan*." said Dai. "I think there'll be a big green light that'll come on and then they'll shout something like 'Go, go, go.' and then you'll jump. Now bear in mind that Tom Hanks won't be on this plane. I've managed to speak to a guy down at Swansea airport who's got a plane but he can't get hold of Tom."

Standing on top of the bale was starting to make me feel a bit dizzy.

"Can we get this over and done with please?" I asked.

"Ok. I'm just waiting for the favourable wind conditions." said Dai, licking his hoof and holding it up to the wind. "Aaaaaaand go, go , go!" he screamed.

This was it.

I closed my eyes and held my breath. And then despite my body screaming out not to jump, I jumped off the bale of hay.

The ground came up to meet me quicker than I thought and in a flash, I had all four hooves back on the ground.

"Ok great." said Dai "Training completed. You're a natural."

***

I lay awake in the barn all night that night. Despite all the other sheep in there, I was the only one who was prepared to do a sky dive to add a bit of excitement to the Royal Welsh Show. Was I the only pioneer on this farm? Was I the only one willing to stick my woolly neck out in the name of entertainment? It wasn't so much that I wanted the attention as such. I'm no Felix Baumgartner and I certainly don't have the backing of Red Bull. But like Felix, I wanted to see if it could be done. He jumped from space and landed on his feet. I wanted to be the first sheep to jump out of a plane and land on his hooves.

The day of the jump came around quicker than I would have liked. I'd had time to prepare physically by jumping off that bale of hay, but I still felt that I could have had more time to prepare mentally.

Farmer Honey loaded Dai and I up into his trailer and we headed off down to Swansea. They dropped me off there and headed on to the Royal Welsh Show in Builth Wells. They were to be my ground crew.

The plane was smaller than I thought it would be. How was THAT going to get us up into the sky? And in fairness, it did struggle to get into the air. The pilot, a short man who went by the name of Glynne Minto (or Glinto Minto as he was referred to by air traffic control) had to use every last yard of the runway to get us airborne.

"Phew." he muttered as we climbed up over the countryside. "Close one that butt."

Although I'd always sat and watched the mountains from my place in the field, I'd never seen anything from the air before. As we pulled up away from the coast and headed inland, I was amazed by the patchwork of fields below us. They didn't seem real. And despite my fear of heights, I didn't feel scared. The drone of the plane's engines seemed to soothe and reassure me. But that didn't last long.

"I'll drop you off at Builth is it butt?" shouted Glynto from the cockpit.

"Aye." I shouted back.

My nerves were beginning to kick in. My stomach started doing somersaults and my anus was starting to twitch.

"Nervous?" shouted Glynto.

"Yes."

"First time?"

"No. I've been nervous lots of times." I replied. I felt that I had to go along with Glynto's reference to post-modern spoof motion pictures about air travel and the disaster genre.

Within half an hour, we were circling the drop zone. Glynto had pressed a button to open the door for me. I knew that waiting down below somewhere, was Farmer Honey and Dai.

I shuffled forward towards the door. It was sure windy out there.

"30 seconds!" Glynto called out.

I shuffled some more.

"Twenty seconds!"

By now, I was stood in the doorway, looking down at the rolling fields. I could see the showground – the people and the animals looked like ants.

"Ten seconds!"

This was it. I pulled down my goggles and got ready to jump.

"Sometimes, you have to come so high to realise how humble we are." I said. "I'm coming home."

"Go, go, go!"

And with that, I jumped.

13 THE GOAT TWINS

Unfortunately for me, I'd spent so long giving my little speech that I was way out over the fields by a few hundred yards. The Royal Welsh Showground was far off in the distance so I had a job to do if I was to land in the centre of the main arena.

The first thing I had to do was open my parachute. I pulled hard on the cord and with a sudden jolt, the 'chute opened and it all went quiet.

The next thing I had to do was to now fly myself back towards the showground. The parachute was quite easy to steer but I was quickly losing height. Down on the ground, I could see the arena and I was able to start making out individuals. I couldn't see Farmer Honey or Dai the Llama. But I knew that they were there. Somewhere.

But I was running out of time. The ground was coming up too fast.

Farmer Honey later described what had happened down in the showground. The main arena had been cleared for my landing and a large crowd had gathered around the barriers. The commentator had announced my plane flying overhead, and the crowd gasped as I leapt. Like some kind of daredevil, I had their fullest attention.

But he said that it was a sorry sight to see me fade away and disappear behind a clump of trees in the distance. The crowd groaned and went back to their business of eating pork rolls and walking large cows around the arena.

Farmer Honey and Dai had to jump in the trailer and head out into the country to find me.

And I arrived back home in the barn a broken sheep.

"How did it go?" asked Dolly.

"I messed up."

"Did you do it?"

"Yes, but I landed in an old woman's back garden." I replied, my head hanging low.

"But you did do it?"

"Yes."

"Well. That's all I need to know. Well done love."

She kissed me on my woolly forehead and trotted out into the field. She was right. I had done it. I was the first quadrupedal, ruminant mammal to have ever jumped from a moving aeroplane and land to earth AND survive.

I went to bed that night with a smile and a ewe on my face. It was Dolly's way of saying 'Well done."

***

A month later we were woken in the night by Dai opening the barn door in the early hours of the morning. His night-vision goggles scanned the barn.

"Everyone ok?" he said.

There were a few grumbles. From the corner of the barn came the sound of a strangled fart.

"No riots in here then?"

No-one answered. There were a few more groans and then Dai closed the door and went back out to patrol the field.

The following morning, I asked Dai why he had come into the barn during the night.

"Riots." he said.

"What do you mean?"

"There's riots. They're kicking off all over the country. They started in London and they're spreading like wildfire. All over the country. There's been looting on a scale unprecedented in modern times."

I didn't quite understand. But sure enough, when I turned on the telly that had been installed in the barn, there were riots on the news.

"If they come round here, I'll…" said Dai.

"You'll what?" I asked.

"I won't be happy." he said.

We'd always been alert to the dangers of foxes entering the farm, but not looters. What would they want from a farm?

Our first night was a nervous one. As the girls lay in the barn, it was left up to myself and Dai to protect the farm. Farmer Honey was on standby with a large sweeping brush handle should Dai call out his alarm signal.

Dai and I never saw each other during the night. We'd devised what we thought was a clever little scheme where we'd walk around the field but at opposite ends so that we could patrol the maximum amount of area each.

But dawn broke and nothing had happened. I spent the day talking gibberish as I'd had no sleep.

Day turned to night and we were on patrol again. But this time, something did happen.

It was in the early hours. From across the field came the piercing alarm call from Dai. In my head, I'd been cwtched up tight in my bed and for a few seconds, the alarm startled me. Getting my head back together, I dashed across the field in the darkness.

I finally got to Dai to see him stood there looking as if he'd just seen a ghost.

"What's happened?" I asked.

Dai didn't answer. I looked around for a clue but there was nothing to suggest that anything had happened.

"Dai. You need to tell me. What's happened?"

Still no reply. By this time, Farmer Honey had come running out of his house with this large sweeping brush handle, shouting at the top of his voice.

"Bloody hoodies! Let me at them!"

He finally got to where Dai and I were stood.

"What's going on?" he asked. "Where's the looters?"

"There are no looters." I said.

"Well what's wrong with this idiot?"

Dai was still stood like a statue, looking far ahead at nothing in particular.

"I don't know." I said. "I've just found him like this." I explained.

"Dai. Dai. Can you hear me?" Farmer Honey slapped Dai around the chops a few times and Dai came-to slightly. He let out a little moan.

"Dai. What did you see?" asked Farmer Honey. He was getting impatient now.

Dai started muttering. "Gloria. Gloria. Gloria." I suddenly felt very cold. Gloria was one of our mob who had been struck by lightning in the field a few months earlier. All that was left of her was four steaming hooves.

"Gloria's gone Dai. She's gone. You know that don't you?" said Farmer Honey. "Come on. Let's get him in."

"But what about the looters?" I asked.

"We'll deal with them if and when they come."

Farmer Honey and I began shuffling poor Dai towards the barn.

"Come on boy." Farmer Honey was doing his best to comfort his guard llama.

It had only been about a minute into our slow journey back to the barn that we saw it.

At first, I thought someone had been shining a torch on us but within seconds, both Farmer Honey and myself turned to the middle of the field.

There, glowing like a large sheep-shaped lightbulb only a hundred yards away was the image of Gloria, the poor sheep who only months earlier, had been vanquished in a flash of light.

"Good God alive!" belted out Farmer Honey. I couldn't say a thing. I was frozen to the spot.

A few seconds later, we both ran screaming into the barn and bolted the door, totally forgetting to bring Dai the Llama with us. We cwtched up to each other and I could feel Farmer Honey shaking all over with fright.

"What will we do? We can't leave Dai out there all night." I said.

"I don't know. I don't know." Farmer Honey's voice was cracking and trembling. "I don't know what to do." We stayed there for a few minutes until we built up the courage to peep around the door.

Slowly, and with a creak that seemed to go on forever, Farmer Honey pulled back the door. We both peered out into the darkness.

We could make out the faint outline of Gloria. She was now fading from view and the light that she was giving off was dimming. Not far away, Dai the Llama was still stood there, still frozen in fear. He was to stay there until first light when Farmer Honey headed out into the field to bring him back into the barn.

***

Dai wasn't in a good way. I'm not sure why it had affected him so badly but it was clear that he wasn't going to be any good as a guard llama.

"I'm going to have to call in some reinforcements." said Farmer Honey, pulling a blanket up tight over Dai as he lay in the barn. "I know who I'm going to call."

Later that day, a truck pulled up at the farm. Farmer Honey went out to meet the driver and a few minutes later, the back door opened and two fierce looking goats, all horn and grimace, stepped off the back. They looked identical. Farmer Honey led them to where I was stood just outside the barn.

"Boys, I'd like you to meet Derek the Weathersheep. He's a worldwide celebrity in his own right. If any looters break in, he's the one you protect first. He's worth his weight in gold." said Farmer Honey.

The goats looked me up and down in complete synchronisation before uttering the words "Yes boss." as if they were one. Then they clicked their back heels and trotted off to the barn where they both took up sentry guard either side of the door. A few of the girls came wandering over to chat to them. It wasn't every day they had two fine specimens to drool over. But the goat twins didn't say a word. They didn't even flinch. They just stood there, stone-faced, looking out over the field.

Famer Honey explained to me that the goats were the twins sons of Gordon the Goat, who stood guard over Dolly the Sheep (the famously cloned one) at the Roslin Institute in the mid-nineties. Their pedigree was never in doubt.

Night fell once again and for me and Dai, it was our first night where we could get our heads down for some proper sleep. It was nice to know that looking after us were two hard-as-nails goats.

As it happened, looters never came to our farm and eventually the goat twins were sent away again. They never said goodbye. Their lorry turned up and they simply clicked their heels and boarded the truck. We never found out where they went and we never heard from them again.

It was a shame as their professionalism would have come in very handy for a dramatic event that took place a few weeks later on a nearby bridge.

14 TINA AND THE BRIDGE

"Don't do it Tina!"

Dolly was calling to her friend Tina, who was stood on a very thin strip of metal on the wrong side of a footpath that led over a high bridge. Down below, jagged rocks and razor sharp rocks cut up out of the grass. Tina wanted to jump and wanted to go out of this world in a grisly way.

"117th!" Tina kept shouting.

"It's ok. We're still ahead of Thailand!" shouted Dolly "And the US Virgin Islands. Stay strong my love!"

For Wales to slip to 117th in the FIFA world rankings was bad enough for Tina but the fact that it came at the hands of a 2-0 defeat to England seemed to make matters worse. Tina was an ardent Wales football fan. She'd once met Gareth Bale at a local fete and promptly fainted.

But today was different. This was a life and death situation. The last thing anyone wanted to see was her jump.

Farmer Honey arrived in his Land Rover.

"What's going on here?" he bellowed, pushing his way past the crowds to the front. He stopped in his tracks when he saw one of his sheep clinging to the railings and a 100ft drop below her.

"What in God's name do you think you are doing you stupid sheep?" he shouted. He was clearly very angry. If she went, it was likely that all the other sheep would follow. That's just the nature of sheep.

"Get your woolly arse back over those railings and back on the farm where you belong!"

But Tina was very distressed.

"117th!" she wailed.

"Look," said Farmer Honey, "We've got Montenegro next. And they're *really* shit. Give the boys a chance to redeem themselves."

There was a tense moment as Tina lurched forward ever so slightly. We all gasped. I knew there was something I HAD to do.

"Tina!" I called out. She turned her head towards me. Tears were rolling down over her woolly face.

"Remember that night we were sat under the stars…?" Dolly, who was stood next to me, cast me a dirty look.

"What night?" asked Dolly.

"Shut up woman." I said with clenched teeth.

"Yes!" said Tina. "Yes, I do!"

"Remember how you told me about your love for Neville Southall and that one day, you'd like to have a lamb and name him Neville?"

The wind was whipping up a treat now and Tina was in real danger of being blown over the side. I had to get through to her.

"Yes! Yes I do!" she said "I was going to call him

Neville and I'd make him grow a bushy moustache and make him wear big green gloves on his front two hooves!"

"That's right Tina. And remember you told me how you'd watch him grow into a fine young ram, and he'd go on to play for Everton Academy and one day go on to play for Wales Sheep Football Team?"

"Yes! Yes I do!" Tina called out.

"Well give little Neville a chance! How will he be able to achieve all those dreams if you jump? He won't even have a chance to make it into the world!"

"117th!" she called out again. She was seriously beginning to get on my tits now.

"Fffffffffffffffffffffffffffffffffffffffffine!" I shouted back. "I've never known such a selfish sheep. Tina this and Tina that. Go on - jump you selfish arsehole."

Suddenly Tina's voice changed.

"Oi! You cheeky sod! What about that time you ate all those carrots that we had delivered over Christmas?" she replied in such a shrill little voice that everyone's ears pricked up.

"I was hungry." I replied. "You ate all the swedes if I remember rightly. No wonder you got such a fat arse."

"Oooo!". Tina's face folded in rage. "I've got a good mind to come over there and smash your face in Derek the Weathersheep!"

"You wouldn't dare," I called back, "You're all mouth you are. Like that time you said you'd been with that goat major – the one who leads on the Welsh rugby team."

As quick as a flash, Tina was back over the railings and chasing me down the street. She caught up with me and gave me a bit of a beating but I'd have rathered that than seeing her spread over a 10 foot radius.

***

From providing weather forecasts to the nation to saving distraught sheep from throwing themselves off bridges, I was beginning to feel more confident about my role on the farm. I was beginning to feel indispensable. The world wouldn't cope without me. And this was to prove the case a few weeks later.

It involved me, my arse, and an SAS sniper.

15. A SHOT IN THE ARSE

It had been a long day down on the farm. It had been one of those lovely crisp autumnal days – those ones where the sun, low in the sky had stretched the shadows of the girls across the field as they made their way back into the barn for the night.

I'd had a good day and was busy monitoring the cloud formations over the mountains before the sun set for the day.

I was just about to head in for the night when it hit me like a bullet.

That's because it was a bullet.

I'd heard the crack of a rifle in the distance just a millisecond before there was a small thud and then the most searing pain I'd ever felt.

It felt like the pain had ripped through my body but I quickly realised that I'd only been shot in the arse. As I was out in the field, far from help, I l knew I had to get back to the barn for help. But I couldn't move.

I glanced around and in the distance, I could make

out three figures, clad in black, scarpering away down the hillside. I'd seen these sort of people before on the telly only a few nights earlier on some documentary. I think they were blowing up some Iranian Embassy or something. I had been impressed by their courage, skill and daring. I was not however, impressed with the bullet they'd just lodged up my arse.

It took me 15 minutes to struggle to the barn. Farmer Honey was soon on hand, administering first aid, dabbing my buttocks with some iodine.

"Those bloody soldiers. Why do they have to come round here practising? Why not Scotland? No-one cares about them lot. It doesn't matter if they shoot any of their sheep."

The pain was unbelievable. Every time Farmer Honey dabbed my arse, it'd send a shooting pain right to the ends of my fleece.

It took a good hour or so for me to be cleaned up and Farmer Honey put me straight to bed. Normally, I wouldn't mind staying in bed all night but this was different. Dolly and Brenda took their places next to me when it came to 'bedtime' but it wasn't the same. There was to be no 'Derek Sandwich' tonight.

***

For a while, Wales had missed out on their daily weather forecasts. If I'm honest, I'm not sure how the country coped. And I felt bad about it.

It took a good few weeks to get me back on my four hooves again but there was one thing that was keeping me going – the Rugby World Cup. I had to watch the opening Wales game lying on my side.

South Africa sneaked a one-point lead to take the first game, but it gave us hope that we could at least be competitive.

Samoa was a pretty tough game but then after sticking some cricket scores on Namibia and Fiji, it was on to the knock-out stages.

Farmer Honey had been ever so good, and had splashed out on a large screen for the barn. He'd also installed two beer pumps and hung up a large Welsh flag at one end of the barn.

The 8th of October was the day we played Ireland. Now don't get me wrong, the Irish are a lovely nation. They're friendly, funny and caring. Except on the rugby pitch. Having been on the wrong end of some green beatings over the years, it was a game I was desperate for us to win.

We did of course. Hoorah! Next up, France.

And within minutes of kicking off against the Frogs, we were in trouble. Captain Sam, our hero of the tournament so far was red-carded for an apparent tip-tackle. The barn fell empty. We couldn't believe it. I've since read what Sam thought about that tackle. He told me that the French guy didn't want to be tackled. And as Sam was such a ferocious tackler, he'd been lifted high in the air. So the French guy pussied it then?

It certainly seemed that way for us watching the rest of the game in the barn. As the game wore on, we became more and more convinced that, despite being down a man, we had a good chance of sneaking it. Justice would be served.

That moment came in the last few minutes of the game. Little short-arse Leigh Halfpenny, who'd been knocked around a bit during the game could save a nation. The whistle had blown for a penalty.

This was it. The moment of glory. Across the world, sports writers hovered over their keyboards, waiting to type the words 'Wales Snatch World Cup Glory'.

Sigh.

Never mind eh?

16 OCCUPY BRECON

Now that people had no more rugby to watch, someone somewhere had the bright idea of 'occupying' certain landmarks worldwide. I believe the idea started in Wall Street in New York where a few people had got themselves some nice tents and pitched them up for the night.

They seemed to be having a whale of a time so it was only a matter of time before people over here wanted a piece of the action. St. Pauls Cathedral in London was chosen in England but it seemed that Wales was to be without one. That was until Farmer Honey decided to host his own one here in Brecon.

Occupy Brecon had a great festival atmosphere about it. Farmer Honey had cleared some land in the field next door and invited some of his farmer friends to come and stay. The first night was a bit threadbare if I'm totally honest. Only Farmer Honey and Mrs Honey were there but soon word got around that fun was to be had.

The best bit about it was that us sheep were

allowed in to the event too. Even though it was only in the field next to ours, it seemed that we were away from the normal humdrum of eating grass and bleating. It was great to let our hair down.

One of the more memorable nights came late on a Saturday. Brenda had been sharing a tent with Dolly and I and we'd all settled down for a good night's sleep. It was a late October night, which can get pretty cold so we were all snuggled up tight.

There were some strange moaning noises coming from a tent nearby which was stopping me falling off to sleep. I could tell it was one of the girls but she seemed to have a ram in with her, probably from the farm next to ours. Put it this way – it sounded like she was lifting some heavy furniture.

It was impossible not to listen to what was going on, but it soon dawned on me that I could hear two male voices with her. This girl was **really** having some fun in that tent!

It was about 15 minutes or so after the noise started that I heard another lad just outside my tent, clearly off his face. I could hear him muttering and falling about all over the place. It was very frustrating. All I wanted to get to sleep. First the girl with the two lads. Now this idiot falling about outside my tent.

I was getting very frustrated. The drunken sheep outside my tent wouldn't go away. I could tell that he'd lost his way and couldn't find his tent.

I had to do something, even if it was to move him on. I sat up, moved towards the tent entrance and unzipped the door. Without saying a word, I popped my head out to see what was going on.

Sure enough, there falling about all over the place was a drunken ram. First he fell to one side. Then he fell to another. For a while, I had flashbacks of the riggwelter I'd tried to save a few years earlier. It was while he was on the floor that this ram stopped for a while and heard the moaning noises coming from the nearby tent.

He slowly got up and made his way gingerly towards the tent. For a second, I thought about warning him about what was going on inside but I suddenly had second thoughts – it'd be much more fun to see what happened.

So I just watched. This is what happened:

The drunken sheep bumbled his way up to the tent, unzipped the door and stuck his head in. There was a brief squeal from the girl and a few mumblings from the lads. The drunken sheep, realising what he'd come across, offered his apologies and zipped the door back up. He still hadn't seen me as he moved away. And he still hadn't seen me as he suddenly stopped in mid-trot, thought for a second, and then headed back to the tent.

He unzipped the door once again and popped his head back in. Through the gap in the doorway, I could clearly see the girl firmly sandwiched between the two rams.

The drunken sheep spoke:

"Any chance of a blow job love?" he asked the girl.

"Piss off!" came the sharp reply "What do you think I am? Some kind of slag?"

The drunken sheep zipped the door shut and slunk off into the night. I zipped mine back up, having had my few minutes of amusement, I was at last ready to get some sleep.

***

Occupy Brecon came to an abrupt end when we were met with some particularly wet weather. I'd forecast it of course so I had headed back to my field but the farmers chose to ignore it as they always do. I had the last laugh.

Christmas was looming large on the horizon. It always seemed the way that some of our animal friends would leave us around Christmas. They'd never tell us they were going. They'd just up sticks and go.

But our Christmas was a quiet one. The fields seemed unnaturally empty during those cold winter days. But the one thing that warmed our hearts was the fact that the Six Nations wasn't too far away.

Grand Slams don't come around very often but when they do, it's always special.

First up – Ireland. Again. How we laughed when Big George bounced off several Irish players to send Jonathan Davies over for a try. How gutted we were when Ireland were six points ahead with just 5 minutes to go. How we jumped with glee when George scored a try in the corner. And how our hearts sank when Halfpenny missed the conversion to win the game with just four minutes on the clock. And how we felt so sorry for that poor Irishman who gave away that penalty to Wales with just a few seconds on the clock.

Did I say 'Feel sorry'?

Sorry. I meant 'ha ha'.

Next was Scotland. Boring.

Then England. Oh yes. England. At Twickenham.

Oof. Now that was a game.

I don't remember much apart from two things.

1. Owen Farrell getting absolutely thumped by Big George. Fair play to Mr Farrell – he got up and dusted himself down as if nothing had happened.
2. and THAT try with just five minutes to go.

And that's all that mattered. There was bedlam in the barn afterwards when we all went loopy. Mrs Honey even invited some of the girls into the farm house and she was a little bemused that some of them knew where her secret stash of biscuits was kept. But it didn't matter. We'd beaten England. The rest of the year could do its worst but we'd still knocked the wheels off the chariot.

The rest of the Six Nations was a bit of a blur, mainly due to the high levels of intoxication and fornication. But that came to an abrupt stop one day when Dolly came out into the field to give me some life-changing news.

17 A BUN IN THE OVEN

"How could you be?"

"It's easy. You mount me, have your bit of fun and erm...that's it." said Dolly.

"And are you sure it's mine?" I asked.

Dolly sighed. "Yeah, thanks. Who else's is it going to be?"

I didn't know what to feel. It only seemed like yesterday that I was a little one, feeling my way into the world. Yet here I was, a few years later, having to face up to the fact that I was to become a dad.

I lay in bed that night staring up at the ceiling of the barn. I couldn't sleep. Question after question ran racing through my head. Would I be a good dad? How was I going to look after it? What if it was ugly? I eventually drifted off in the early hours but awoke before dawn to find Dolly poking me in the back with one of her hooves.

"What do you want?"

"I'd like a drink please." she replied.

"Well you know where the trough is." I said. I just

wanted to go back to sleep.

"Derek! I'm pregnant!"

This was the first of a tough few weeks for me. The thing is, she'd been pregnant for nearly four months now and she hadn't even noticed (I'm not saying she was a big girl. Actually, yes I am). The list of daily chores grew by the day. Luckily Dolly never went through that funny stage of eating rubbish but she was getting a little bit lazy around the farm. Yes ok, she was carrying my little one within her. But there was no need for her to commandeer the barn's only TV remote control and there certainly wasn't any need to fart very loudly whenever she wanted 'just because she was pregnant'. And boy did they stink. Hormonal farts always do.

When the day finally came, it was pretty much a straightforward labour. I think Dolly thought she was going to do another one of her thick hormonal farts again, but in fact, it was a little lamb who popped out and landed flat on his back.

Dolly gave him a good licking to stimulate him and to wake him and with a few minutes, he was up on his unsteady feet, juddering around the field. I was gobsmacked. How could I have produced such an amazing little thing?

Dolly didn't seem too fazed by it all. She called him to us but I still couldn't speak. It seemed that her maternal nature just 'kicked in'. She pointed to the mess of blood and fanny batter on the floor.

"I'm not coming round picking up your mess after you. I want you to clear that all away or no telly tonight." she said and trotted off back to the barn.

The little lamb came over to me and nuzzled into me.

"Don't go getting any funny ideas around here sunshine. There ain't no tit to be had here." I told him. I felt that I had to assert my authority as a father. But as I looked down at his little wet furry face, I couldn't feel anything other than pure love. He was my son. My boy.

"I'm going to call you Spartacus." I told him.

He let out a little 'Baa' and then hopped on into the barn in the search for some milk. As I had found out when I was a nipper, milk was vital to a little one in the first few hours and I followed him in to make sure he got some. Last thing I wanted was a case of the scours while I was watching Eastenders.

***

Those first few days were very special. Spartacus slept when he should have and was a dream during his waking hours. But then after that, he started getting cheeky and became very demanding. I had to tread the fine line between showing him love and laying down the law. Having no father of my own, I found it hard to judge so I thought that I'd play both roles in a good cop/bad cop situation, just to keep him on his toes and to maintain some balance. Some days he'd ask me if he could go out and play in the field and sometimes I'd say yes. Then some days he'd ask the same question and I'd tell him where to stick his stupid ideas.

But there was an episode where I'd severely regret not being tough on him.

It was a lovely yellow spring day and Sparty had been bugging me all morning to go and play with all the other lambs at the bottom of the field. They were all having a 'Bouncing Party' where they'd put some Tom Jones on the stereo and bounce around the field like lambs are supposed to do.

I was having a 'good cop' day and sent him on his way. I had a few forecasts to look at in any case so thought it'd be best off all round if he was out with his mates.

After an hour or so, Johnny lamb came running up to me as I was sat consulting some charts.

"Is Spartacus coming out to play today?" he said in his little squeaky voice.

"He went down about an hour ago." I never really like Johnny. He'd done nothing wrong but his mother smelt like a piss and he always had a snotty nose.

"Where?" Johnny said. He turned and scanned the field.

"He went down over that way." I said without looking up.

"Can't see him." said Johnny.

I looked up. He was right. There was an empty patch of field where I had last seen Sparty. My chest tightened.

"Well where is he?" I asked.

"That's what I came to ask you." said Johnny.

"Don't get cheeky with me." I wasn't in the mood for insolence.

I looked around the field again. Nothing. The lambs I had presumed were with Sparty had moved up the field and were now playing the 'Sitting in a Field Doing Nothing' game.

"Shit." I said, dropping my charts and darting off down the field. Again, nothing. Panic was gripping me hard now. Running back up the field, I started calling out his name. Other sheep were looking at me as if I was stupid. But I didn't care. I had to find Spartacus.

Several hours later, he hadn't been found and night was drawing in. Farmer Honey had called a meeting in the barn. He was hoping to do one last search before night fell.

He unravelled a map of the field and laid it on a bale of hay. The field was large square so it'd be pretty easy to cover. What I was worried about was whether Spartacus had fallen into a ditch. Or worse still, taken by a fox.

Four teams stretched out over the field to the far corners. Farmer Honey jumped onto his tractor and fired up the engine. Slamming it into first gear, he roared off down the field like some bucking bronco. I went looking in some bushes for a third time.

I felt helpless. Totally helpless. I wanted to be everywhere all at once. Out there, somewhere, was my little boy.

Night slowly crept in and I was finding it hard to breathe. Dolly was out with the girls, scouring all the hedgerows nearby. The bright headlights of Farmer Honey's headlamps almost blinded me as he chugged back up to the farm house and cut the engine. It shuddered to a stop.

Farmer Honey slowly stepped off the tractor and made his way over to me.

"Can't find him anywhere." he said. "Come on. Let's go in." He ushered me to the barn but I knew I had to keep on looking. He was out there somewhere.

Just then, there came a loud squeal from inside the farmhouse – the sort of loud squeal that we'd hear from the farmhouse when Mrs Honey found a Daddy Longlegs in her bedroom and then lost it as she tried to bash it with her slipper.

"Stay here." said Farmer Honey and he flew at the house.

It was while I was trying to clear my muddled mind and decide what I was going to do next that the farm door flew open and Farmer Honey emerged, carrying little Spartacus aloft over his head.

"He's here!!!" he cried.

My heart bulged. I was hit by a tsunami of emotion, and struggling to my feet, I scampered across to be reunited with my little one. His face was all dirty and he smelt a bit.

"Had his head stuck down our outside shitter." said Farmer Honey.

***

The rest of spring was relatively uneventful. The summer weather was picking up and every day, Spartacus was getting bigger and stronger.

It was fair to say that little Sparty was becoming a bit of a handsome hunk and it's also fair to say that he was taking after his father. Yet Sparty was a bit more sporting than his old man.

I think it was the Olympics that really inspired him to sporting greatness. He'd sit watching the games every night and every night, he'd turn to me and say:

"I'd like to be able to say to people that I run quite fast for a living." or "I'd like to be able to say to people that I jump quite far for a living."

Spartacus's dreams of glory was about to come true when Brenda came up with the rather splendid idea of the Sheep Games which were held on the last week of August.

Fair play to the old girl, she'd really thought it through. We had a wealth of competitions here at the farm, ranging from 'Running as Fast as You Can' to 'Jumping as Far as You Can' and even a 'How Loud Can You Bleat' competition. Spartacus, as expected, excelled in all areas of the games (apart from the 'How Far Can You Spread Your Legs Competition' which was won by Brenda), sitting proudly at the top of the medal winners' table. It was the proudest moment of my life.

18. UPWARDS AND ONWARDS

I would have loved to have started this final chapter by saying that I've really enjoy writing my autobiography but to be totally honest, it's been a pain in the arse. It's meant long nights and early mornings. I've missed out on lots of nookie with Dolly (and Brenda) and lots of nights on the sheep wine. I'm only doing it to because I want my story to be told and to make a bit of money so that I can buy Spartacus some decent daps for when he starts Sheep School next year. I'd hate to have to send him in wearing Plimsolls.

I guess now that I've told my story so far, I can go back to forecasting the weather, especially now that the winter months are wrapping their dark arms around us.

I'll write another autobiography of course when I've done enough interesting things to talk about, like Katie Price did. I won't include stories of Peter Andre in it though because, to be frank, I find him quiet boring.

In the meantime, it'll be back to my day job and back to Facebook. Facebook is a funny old thing. Every morning, if I'm not otherwise engaged with Dolly and Brenda, I'll get up and publish my weather forecast for the day. Having so many Facebook friends, it's easy to get distracted from my day job. I enjoy reading everyone's statuses, and feel good about my life when I read the moaning of others.

I've had a good life so far. I have the love of a good woman and good friends. I have an amazing talent and I have a beautiful son in Spartacus. Yes, life has its challenges now and then, but that's normal. That's life. Deal with it.

I'll continue to post my weather updates if I can be arsed. If you're on Facebook and you aren't already on my friends list, drop me a request.

I accept anybody these days.

I always have.

A WOOLLY YARN

ABOUT THE AUTHOR

Derek The Weathersheep lives on a Rex Honey's Farm high in the Brecon Beacons, South Wales.

From his high vantage point, Derek can cast his sheep's eye across the whole of South Wales, and forecast the South Walian population about forth-coming weather events.

He first caught the meteorological bug when he was just a lamb. He was the first sheep to correctly forecast the great snows of 2006, when he ran to Farmer Honey's house, woke him from his slumber, bleated for a bit, and then led Farmer Honey to the rest of the sheep who were about to be cut off from the farm by the drifts. 48 sheep were rescued that night. Farmer Honey rewarded him by presenting him with the Freedom of Honey Farm.

Derek's girlfriend, Dolly (not to be confused with the famous cloned one- they just look alike) is the best looking ewe on the field, and constantly draws attention from male sheep and sometimes even other female sheep. Juan the LoveSheep, a Spanish import, brought by Farmer Honey, to increase virility in the flock, constantly tries to woo Dolly, much to Derek's dismay and amusement.

Find Derek at www.weathersheep.com

Printed in Great Britain
by Amazon.co.uk, Ltd.,
Marston Gate.